Designed For Victory

Daily Practical and Spiritual Wisdom for Winning Life Battles

Kennedy King Odimba

Dedication

I want to dedicate this book to my Lord and Savior, Jesus Christ, and to my son, Brandon U. Odimba, whose presence in my life has continually motivated me to strive for a better future.

Acknowledgements

I would like to acknowledge the remarkable individuals who partnered with me in bringing this book to life. Their support came in many forms: proofreading, offering constructive feedback, and helping me refine the title and overall vision of this work.

I am deeply grateful for their time, insight, and encouragement throughout this journey.

My heartfelt appreciation goes to Uchenna Ugwu, Tosin Ade, exceptionally good friends of mine; Wisdom Ogbonna, my cousin; and Fidelis Obuzo, a close and trusted friend. For helping me refine the Title of this book.

I am especially thankful to Justice Orisakwe for his professional advice throughout the making of this book. And for taking out time from his busy schedule to write the Forwarding.

My greatest thanks go to my parents, Mr. Julius Odimba and Mrs. Blessing Odimba, whose constant prayers, encouragement, and unwavering belief in me have been a source of strength and motivation.

And not forgetting everyone else who has supported this work, both directly and indirectly. May this book stand as a legacy and a shared fruit that we will all live to enjoy.

Thank you all so much.

Foreword

By Justice N. Orieukwu (Chaplain Intern) at Vanderbilt university Nashville, Tennessee.

Some books simply share information. Others change how we see ourselves. Designed for Victory is the kind of book that speaks to the heart.

From the very beginning, Kennedy writes with honesty shaped by real life, not theory. His stories are personal, thoughtful, and deeply human. They reflect lessons learned through struggle, faith, and growth. As you read, it feels less like being taught and more like walking beside someone who understands your journey.

Each chapter offers encouragement and hope. Even in moments of doubt, this book reminds us that we are never without strength or direction. Kennedy challenges us to look again at our words, our dreams, our fears, and our purpose, not as limits, but as opportunities. At its core is a powerful truth: God has placed possibility and purpose within every one of us.

What makes this book special is its clarity. The message is simple, sincere, and easy to understand. The scriptures included are not heavy or overwhelming; they are gentle reminders meant to guide and strengthen.

They show that faith is not distant or unreachable, but present in our everyday lives.

As you read, you may find yourself stopping, not because the words are difficult, but because they feel familiar. You may recognize your own experiences, your own struggles, and your own hopes reflected in these pages. And in those moments, you may be reminded that you can rise again, that you are stronger than you think, and that you were created for more.

This book is ultimately about awakening. Victory is not something we stumble into by chance; it is something we are designed for. Within every person is a resilience that often appears during life's hardest moments. Kennedy's words help bring that strength to the surface.

I offer this foreword with gratitude for the courage it took to write this book and for the courage it will inspire in its readers. May these pages renew your hope, strengthen your faith, and remind you that even when your progress feels unseen, God is still at work.

Read slowly. Reflect honestly. And move forward with confidence. You were designed for victory.

Preface

This book was inspired by my deep and enduring desire to make a meaningful impact in the lives of others. For as long as I can remember, I have been preoccupied with a simple but powerful question: How can my life leave someone else better than I found them? How can a conversation, an interaction, or even a brief moment of connection become a blessing to someone I encounter each day? These questions have continually shaped my thinking and driven me to explore ideas, principles, and practical ways to use my gifts to positively influence others.

This passion is what gave birth to Designed for Victory. I want to submit to you, I mean you, that is reading this book right now, that you are truly designed for victory.

God has created you with everything you need to be a blessing to the world around you. You are not lacking, and you do not need anything else to complete your life.

The main purpose of this book is to leave you better than before, to help you recognize and appreciate all that God has already deposited within you. That is my greatest desire and the driving force behind this work.

I encourage you to read this book attentively and thoughtfully. Each chapter offers insight, practical steps, and wisdom designed to equip you for daily life. My hope is that these pages will strengthen you, guide you, and prepare you to face life with confidence and purpose.

Life will undoubtedly present challenges, obstacles, and unexpected hurdles. Yet I want to remind you that your Creator-God, who reigns in heaven, has already equipped you for this journey called life. You are victorious. You are not alone. I want you to know that I care about you, and more importantly, God cares about you. You matter. Your life matters. You are not here by accident-you complete this world.

May this book be a source of hope to you, a light at the end of the tunnel, and a catalyst for a renewed mindset and fresh perspective. I firmly believe that for things to change, you must first change. My prayer is that this book becomes the change you have been seeking-the shift that renews your mind, lifts every limitation before you, and empowers you to live beyond boundaries.

I hope to cross paths with you one day and have you share your testimony of how this book blessed your life. Until then, I wish you a meaningful and transformative reading experience.

Happy reading.

Contents

Introduction

"Above everything else, I would like to start you on this wonderful journey by reminding you that you are wonderfully and fearfully made and equipped by God to be victorious in this life."

Psalms 139:14

In other words, there was a high level of intentionality, carefulness and detailed processes that were followed to bring about your existence on this Earth. You are not just some random specimen that was made from trial and error, you are not a surprise to God, he molded and designed you to be victorious in this life.

The Bible said he knew you even before you were formed in your mother's womb. - Jeremiah 1:5 - My earnest hope is that you will get to discover more of who God has made you as you read through the pages of this book.

This book is a compilation of short stories, philosophical quotes, biblical References, and daily loads of wisdom to help you face and thrive through life challenges in everyday life.

These short stories were birthed from my personal experiences and some special individuals I have met and read about over the years.

Hence, the efficacy of gaining profound wisdom is crucial if we must make any significant progress in our daily lives, that's why the Bible in the book of Proverbs (4:7-9) said: Wisdom is the principal thing; therefore get wisdom: and with all thy getting get understanding.

One big question that always comes to my mind each time I go through any kind of life challenges or special occurrences in my life, is the big question of What can I learn from this? In what way can I use this knowledge to change the perspective of a larger group of people in a more meaningful and positive way?

Hence, it is not what we go through in life that changes our life, but what we learn from it that does.

We are constantly bombarded by life pressures, fear of the future, negative news from the media, and even fear of the upcoming economic recession, which has been so much been talked about in the news and across different internet blogs, coupled with the war currently going on in Iran. That has stimulated a lot of tension and fear of not knowing what is next for the economy with gas prices and food spiking up every day.

It is obvious that if we don't begin to intentionally reprogram and deprogram our minds with more and more positive and uplifting messages, what happens is that people will eventually get overwhelmed, which will in turn lead to depression, anxiety, fears, and even mental blocks that tend to limit us from living out our true potentials.

The main purpose of this book, therefore, is to remind ourselves that even in the midst of a broken world, there is still a lot of hidden good out there to be experienced. In other words, by changing the way we look at things, the things we look at will begin to change.

You see, the bigger problems we face are not really the obvious events and facts that are happening around us every day; the bigger problems, however, are the interpretation and meaning we attach to them.

The way you see or perceive a particular problem in your life will determine whether you find a solution for it or let it overwhelm you.

Wrapped up in the chapters ahead are life-changing stories, lessons, quotes, uncommon wisdom, and even biblical references to build up your mental strength and help you navigate each day with confidence.

This is a book I would recommend you read and re-read every day for more clarity and understanding, it's more like a daily devotion to jump-start your day.

I want to encourage you to pick up your highlighter, note pads, and join me in this journey as I reveal this uncommon knowledge and life-changing principles to help you change your perspective and outlook on life, so you can begin facing every day with more confidence and courage.

It's time to level up!

Winning Wisdom 1: You Are Superior to Your Circumstances

"Most of the important things in the world have been accomplished by people who had kept on trying when there seemed to be no hope at all."

Dale Carnegie

The phrase you are superior to your circumstances has been spoken and written about in several articles and journals. It is a mindset of champions; it is a mindset that keeps you going from failure to failure without getting discouraged. Nothing is more liberating than the conviction and understanding that you are stronger than whatever life may throw at you, and you actually are! It makes no difference what you might be going through, even as you are reading through the chapters of this book, it will all come to pass when you stay focused and refuse to give up.

That's why I have chosen to make it our winning wisdom number one in this book because, you have to wake up every day with this believe and conviction that you are stronger, smarter and way more powerful than whatever life may throw at you, one of my favorite verses in the Bible is (Philippians 4:13, it says: I can do all things through Christ who strengthens me.

That is a very remarkable statement, notice it does not say some things; it says all things. What this means is that the human spirit is created and wired to triumphantly face any kind of life circumstances.

You see, you may not be able to control the rain, the storms, or what you may call the winters of life, but you have the power to control what you will do after the storm is over.

Put in another way, life is 10% what happens to you and 90% what you do about it; in other words, you and only you will get to choose whether to let your circumstance defeat you or inspire you to create a new standard for what is possible by the human mind.

And it is important to note that some of the greatest discoveries of human history have all been born out of men and women who choose to courageously turn their adversities into possibilities and even opportunities.

Hence, this brings me to a very interesting story shared by a writer about a certain young athlete, whose shoes accidentally pulled off from his feet in the middle of a very competitive race, but this young athlete did not let that incident or setback deter his commitment to continue with the race.

Instead, he went back, picked up his shoes, put them back on his feet, and continued with the race. Keep in mind that the time did not stop running because of what had happened to him.

But surprisingly, he pulled out one of the most fascinating records in the history of track and field, when he ran back and still managed to beat his fellow competitors who had gone far ahead of him in the race, and still ended up the winner of the race in normal time.

He refused to let the time lost, delays, and noise from the crowd stop him from running to the finish line and ultimately winning the medal.

This story can be linked to your own personal pursuit of your life goals and purpose. You are going to face times when things will not go exactly the way you planned them. Just remember that a bend in the road is not a reason to stop your journey; it is just a time to reorganize, brainstorm, and discover an even better and smoother route to your destination.

Never give up! You are stronger than your circumstances!

Key Important Lesson

You must keep pushing forward even in the midst of setbacks, mistakes and failures because it is often your hardest times that will give birth to the most beautiful moments of your life.

Biblical Reflection:

When you pass through the waters, I will be with you, and when you pass through the rivers, they will not sweep over you. When you walk through the fire, you will not be burned; the flames will not set you ablaze.

-Isaiah 43:2-

Winning Wisdom 2: Become stronger!

"Do not wish things were easier, wish you were better, do not wish for less problems, wish for more wisdom."

Jim Rohn.

I have come to the realization that life does not get easier, but you and I have the power to get better, get smarter, change our lives, improve, grow, and thrive, no matter how difficult it might get.

In other words, you have the power to wake one day and decide to completely change the direction of your life; that is the most powerful attribute we all have as humans.

Hence, some changes are forced upon us by life circumstances, while some are deliberately created and acted upon by ourselves. But sadly, the former kind of change can even destroy you if not acted upon thoughtfully.

The letter, however, is my focus in this chapter, because the best kind of change is the change that happens when you want to change, not the kind of change that happens when you must change. Hence, this conversation brings to the very profound advice Author and writer Spencer gives in his famous book titled, "Who Moved My Cheese."

In his book, "Who Moved My Cheese" Author Dr. Spencer Johnson, narrates a very instructive story on how various individuals react to change in their lives and how we can manage Change more effectively.

Change is inevitable, and we are all going to face it at some point in our lives.

The biggest question, however, is the response and the approach on which we choose to handle it. Spencer's advice is centrally based on approaching Change with an optimistic mindset, knowing that everything we have is temporary.

He teaches us to be flexible with life and to never get complacent with where we are or what we have accomplished.

He tries to remind us that there is always something better than what we are currently experiencing right now. In fact, if we do all we are capable of doing, we will literally amaze ourselves.

My questions for you right now are, why settle for less when you were created to accomplish more? What would you do differently today if you were not afraid?

So, you see, life is like riding a bicycle; the moment you stop pedaling, you will start falling as well. We are living in one of the most fascinating times in human existence, where most of the things we know are becoming obsolete, if we must therefore remain relevant in these changing times, we also have to make a deliberate decision to grow, learn, improve and evolve!

Here is my point, if you don't like your Job, change it, if you don't like your body weight change it, if you don't like your city, then move to a new city, you are not a tree is as easy as it sounds, but very few people actually realize this because they are procrastinating or maybe waiting for a perfect time or a perfect moment, but that perfect moment is an illusion, there is never going to be a perfect day or perfect time to begin changing your life, you and only you have the power to make this moment your perfect moment, yet a lot of folks are very good about wishing for things to change, they might make statements like, I do wish i can wake up one day and all my problems will disappear or I do wish all my dreams can happen this month or this year, but that's the problem, you don't wish for things to happen, you work for things to happen, you study, learn, commit and take massive actions for things to change, you don't shy away from your problems and wish they will change one day, no! You must face them squarely and brainstorm on new ways and ideas to solve them.

The book of Ecclesiastes 4:11 makes it more profound; if you wait for perfect conditions, you will never get anything done.

So, it's time to start adding value to your life, and when I say value, I mean knowledge, read new books, learn new skills, attend new programs, connect with more quality people, conduct more research in your area of expertise, and become better! You have to make a decision to become stronger, smarter and even richer, for that's the only true way to remain relevant in this time of massive change and transformation.

Never let the fear of change hinder you from going to where you would have succeeded, instead let it drive you to discover new territories and opportunities for your journey! You are capable of more! Do not settle for less!

Key Important Lesson

While life never gets easier for anyone, we can however, grow stronger, become better and smarter by intentionally deciding to consistently add value to our lives and even gain new skills to remain relevant and competitive in a changing world.

Biblical Reflection:

I count not myself to have apprehended, but this is one thing I do, forgetting those things which are behind, and reaching forth unto those things which are before, I press toward the mark of the high calling of God in Christ Jesus.

-Philippians 3:13-14-

Winning Wisdom 3: The Power Hour

"If you don't design your own life plan, chances are you'll fall into someone else's plan. And guess what they have planned for you? Not much."

Jim Rohn

The way you start your day, mostly the first hour of your day, will determine how the rest of the day turns out.

Your power hour can be described as the first two hours of every new day given to you by God, you see, every day you see the rising of the sun is like a gift given to you by God, and your only gift back to him, is making a decision to maximize every second, minute and hours of that day, in other words your main purpose should be to produce some kind of meaning and positive impact in appreciation to God, simply put, "make each day count.

Key questions to ask at the beginning of your day,

1. How can I make better use of my time today?

2. What is one thing that I can do right now that will bring about a greater impact in my list of priorities?

3. In what way can my life contribute towards the realization of a better community and even a better

world for everyone?

It is therefore pertinent to understand that the way you start your first few hours every day will set the tone for the rest of the day, and that is why you must develop what I call a morning ritual.

The concept of the power hour is a concept I discovered in my college days and have practiced it over and over again in all these years. These same practices have helped me set up my own productive daily routine that supports my daily life goals, and I believe it will do the same for you.

The biggest thing to note however, is that this is one principle that sets the difference between those who merely want something and those who are committed to what they want.

Hence, the big question is, could getting up one hour earlier each day be the one key that unlocks all your potential goals? Could staying up a little bit late at night while working on some personal projects when everyone else is asleep, be the one catalyst that accelerates your dreams?

Yes, it could, and that is why treating your first one each day with optimal priority and staying up say one hour longer or even two hours longer could push you further into your desired goals faster than you would ever imagine. Let me tell you a little story about how this simple change in my own daily routine changed my life some years ago.

Three years ago, when I joined the United States army, during my basic training experience, my first week was very hectic, and really overwhelming due to the intense pressure put on us by the Drill Sergeants, statically speaking the first and second week of basic training is usually when most recruits quit because of the intense pressure to complete huge tasks with little or no time for recovery.

The goal is usually to test your mental strength to determine how you can manage pressure.

It got to a point when I found it extremely hard to even complete a 2 Mile run, I was on the verge of quitting on myself, but something changed when I began listening to the drill sergeants.

I can still remember vividly one of the conversations I had with one of the drill sergeants, where he shared how minor changes in my daily routine can result in huge improvements in my overall performance and fitness level.

He went on to emphasize how some minor changes in waking up early, prepping and preparing for each day can help change my results.

I have one of the sergeants actually approached me personally and he was like Trainee, as we were usually addressed, he said I so much believe in you and believe you are going to eventually pull through your shortcomings and become the best soldier you were meant to be, these words of encouragement, went straight to my heart and helped me regained confidence in myself but in-spite of all those words of encouragement the first week came and passed but was still struggling, with completing my runs within the expected time allotted for it to be completed, but one important thing that happened was that boast in my confidence and a belief in myself.

Hence, the second week came, and I was still struggling, but by the third week, something happened, I started waking up at least 30 minutes early to run by myself, in those early cold hours of the morning.

So, when I got up in the morning, I would splash some ice-cold water on my face to get me fully awake, I would read something positive and say my prayers, and this time my colleagues would still be asleep, so I would just go out in the field and just run for like 30 minutes.

I did that for the first three days, and on the fourth day, something automatically switched. I noticed that my 2-mile completion time went from 23 minutes to 16 minutes.

And this was something that I had been struggling to complete in 23 minutes. Hence, the big question here is what really changed?

Well, to answer that, the change happened because I changed.

Because I started changing some little habits, tiny things like getting up early and priming my time, so this is what the power hours can really do in our life, minor changes in the things we do first in the morning can bring about huge changes in our results.

Here is my point, I want you to look at something in your life that you really want to change by changing little habits and mastering the effective use of your power hour, i.e your first few hours when you get up each day.

I strongly suggest you start applying this to any area in your life where you desire tremendous change, by acknowledging and applying this principle, you will begin to see yourself transformed in ways you can never imagine and you will eventually begin to complete tasks you never thought were initially possible.

I hope this story resonates with you, and I hope it helps you bring about that needed change for your next level in life. In other words, by mastering the first couple of hours of your morning, you can completely transform the outcome of your life.

Key Important Lesson:

If you are ever going to see tremendous change in your life, it's going to take your ability to change the way you manage the first couple of hours of each day that you wake up.

You have to come up with a ritual, you have to come up with a routine, you have to decide to master your first hour. It's not a time to rush to your phone, it's not a time to make any kind of unplanned calls is a time to really prime yourself to prepare yourself for the day when you get up in the morning make your prayers, splash cold water on your face or do something to help you get up fully, pick up a pen and set your priorities for the day if possible go for a run, read something positive to super charge your mind and start with the most hardest set of goals on your list for that day.

Fundamentally, if there is nothing else you learned from this chapter, I want you to never forget that your first hour of the day is your key to transforming your life. Master this and master your life.

Prayer

Never start a new day without first inviting the one who gives you the day to direct your path. Prayer is very powerful because you are involving the supernatural to rule over the natural. It makes everything easy.

Biblical Reflection:

Commit to the Lord whatever you do, and he will establish your plans

-Proverbs 16:3-

Winning Wisdom 4: What Others Think Does Not Matter

"Is not about changing what people think about you, it is about changing what you think about yourself."

Mel Robbins

You have to stop giving much concern about what other people think about your life, we live in a world where we are constantly looking for validation for what somebody else think about us, for example, when you are trying to make a simple decision like what to say in a meeting, a decision of what to post on your social media space, a decision to choose who to marry or be friends with.

The list goes on and on. The truth is that you cannot control what other people think about you, trying to do that is a waste of your precious energy.

Some people even bother about thoughts like, "What if people don't like what I'm doing? What if no one supports my dream? What if my friends don't like my outfit?" And this is sabotaging yourself from living out your authentic life and making authentic decisions of what you want out of life, it is very pertinent to realize that, you can never control what other people think about you, because it doesn't matter whether you do something or do nothing, people are always going to have an opinion about what you should have done and what you did wrong.

Think of a time when you wanted to go to an event, or you wanted to attend a special occasion, and maybe you chose the clothes and shoes you wanted to wear, and you looked at yourself in the mirror; right in your own eyes, you looked good for yourself.

You looked at your outfit, you looked at your hairstyle and your makeup, and everything appeared good to you, but just when you wanted to step out of the house, a second thought came into your mind, and you thought to yourself saying, "What will people think about my hairstyle? What will they think about my makeup? What would they think about my shoes? You probably ended up changing something in your dressing just because of what somebody else would think. And I am not saying you should not try to look your best self, but you should not do it to be liked or appreciated by others. Do it because it feels good for you!

And that's the point I am trying to make, you just decided to change who you are just to please somebody else thought of you, which is completely beyond your control, just a few minutes ago, you were very much pleased by your outfit after checking out yourself in the mirror but now you completely forgot how good you looked rather prefer to change everything to please someone else perception of you.

My question is, how long are you going to keep living your life based on people's thoughts and opinions?

How long are you going to keep sabotaging your life based on what someone else thinks of you?

You see, one of the biggest things I've discovered in life is that no matter what you do, you are never going to please everybody. It was the philosopher "William James" who said, "I don't know any secret to success but one sure way to failure, is trying to please everyone."

Here is my point, whether you do something or do nothing, people are always going to say something. The earlier you realize that, the better for you.

You cannot control what people think or say about you, but can you control what you believe about yourself by just being who you are, and embracing yourself, and that includes your imperfections, because that is what makes you human in the first place.

Here is my point again, there are very little things you can control in life, you can control your response and attitude after something has happened to you, but you literally have no control over what will happen or what people are going to do or say about you afterwards in other words, what you think about yourself, how you respond to things around you, these are all under your control one thing that is beyond your control is what someone else thinks of you or what other people say about you, you cannot control it and since you cannot control it while letting it stop you from living your authentic life.

Get unstuck

It's time to get unstuck, it's time to wake up, it's time to start living your true, authentic life, it's time to rise up and be unapologetically who you are! It's time to stop striving to fit in, you were created to be original, stop trying to die a photocopy.

Take control of your emotions

It's time to take control of the emotions of your mind, of who you are. It's time to tell yourself I am in control of my life. I am the author of my own destiny. I am good enough. I am strong enough. I am smart enough. My relevance is not based on people's validation of my ability; my relevance is based on doing what is in line with my purpose.

A lot of times we try to live our life to please people to please the society to please our family members while sabotaging our own authentic self, but let today be for you that reminder that you are enough the way you are, your ideas are worthwhile, your thoughts are valid, you are unique and not everyone is supposed to like or appreciate you and that's okay.

Here is a little story about what happened when I took my son to the park earlier in the month:

I was in the park with my son, where I took him to play with some of his friends. While he was playing with his friends, I had this magazine that I was reading while also watching him play with his friends, and after they had played for about an hour or so, I remembered I had an appointment that I needed to take care of.

So, at once I called his attention and said, Brandon I have an appointment, so we are going to be leaving soon, okay? But he hesitated, saying, Daddy please can you give me more time?

And said ok I'm going to give you ten more minutes to play and we'll be leaving okay, he said daddy ok and hurriedly went and tell his friends that he will be living soon and as he went I immediately noticed that among all his friends he was playing with there was one particular one that he got so acquainted with and he specifically told that one, saying my daddy said we're going to be leaving in ten minutes but I don't know if I will still recognize you when I see you next time.

Those words immediately drew my attention to their conversation and made me curious to hear the little five-year-old's response.

The little five-year-old replied, saying, "I don't think so, you will still know me when you see me next time because there is no one that looks like me." In my mind, I was like, "Wow, how did she get to know that?" And I talked to myself, "What a reply by this little five-year-old, how in the world did she come about that statement: 'No one else looks like me.' I was like Wow, where did she learn that from at her young age?

Well, I narrated that story to further buttress my point of how unique we are innately wired, even from our early childhood.

That's the way we were all originally wired by the creator himself, but as we mature in age, our desire to conform to the norms of the world and our environment tends to get the better of our original identity of being who we are meant to be, we are therefore carried away by the desire to be liked and accepted by others, we are constantly seeking to fit in, or liked by others in other to feel accepted but that in turn robs us of our biggest power which lies in our own uniqueness and being ourselves.

I hope for this to be a reminder to you today that you were created differently to fulfill your own unique purpose on this earth, in other words, your ultimate power lies in your uniqueness and in being who you are born to be, not trying to be like or look like anyone else.

Hence, your power and authentic self comes alive when you choose to live your life irrespective of what anybody else thinks about you.

Let this be a reminder that you are here to fulfill a unique purpose, that you are here on a unique mission, that you are here because the Creator Himself knew you from the outset and formed you for your own unique assignment in the world. You were never meant to fit in; you were made to stand out.

Is pertinent to note that, your height, your color, your facial expression, your personality, in fact, everything about your life was crafted the way it is because of your unique mission

And it is pertinent to also note that there is no stereotype to success, or a certain thing you should do or must be considered successful,

Success for me is living and fulfilling your own unique assignment, and that could be making your own Artwork it could be producing your own music or even raising successful kids that change the world for good.

Simply put, success is fulfilling your own unique calling

Make a decision today, to start living your life based on your own unique purpose. Never settle for the idea of trying to please people because you can never control what other people think or how they are going to feel about you but you can always control what you think about yourself and what you bring to the world.

You matter, your thoughts matter, your ideas matter. Your power lies in standing up for what you believe about yourself, not what others think about you. You are incomparable.

Key Important Lessons:

1. Above everything else is pertinent to note that you don't have control over what others think or say about you, so do what makes you happy.

2. Since you know that no matter what you do, people are always going to say something, you might as well do what makes sense to you and gives your life a sense of fulfillment.

3. Your goal in life is not to be liked by everyone; your ultimate goal is to do what is in line with your life purpose.

4. Do not be consumed by the thought of what others think about you; that is beyond your control, and the more you do that, the more you are wasting energy you could channel into doing something more productive with your time on this earth. Step out of that slow lane today.

5. Stop focusing on changing what people say or think about you, instead focus on changing the way you think about yourself.

Finally, brothers and sisters, whatever is true, whatever is noble, whatever is right, whatever is pure, whatever is lovely, whatever is admirable-if anything is excellent or praiseworthy-think about such things.

Philippians 4:8-

Winning Wisdom 5: Your Words are Seeds

"Kind words can be easy and short to say, but their echoes last a lifetime."

Mother Teresa

The power and impact of what we say every day cannot be overemphasized. It is therefore pertinent to note that our words are seeds; the things we say daily can either make or destroy us. The world we live in was created by words of the mouth; so also, every day you live, you are either creating or destroying your life through what you say.

Hence, in this chapter, my main aim is to help you understand how powerful your confessions, the words you say to yourself and even to others, are in determining the results you will eventually get out of life.

Your words are powerful and it goes a long way in determining the outcome of your life.

A little story about myself, growing up in Nigeria so many years ago I can still remember when I would tell my friends I do like to travel to the United States of America one day, I do like to go over there and study and explore different cultures and have a change of life, I also remember telling one of my friend one day I would like to be rich, I would like to be an author, I would like to one day join the United States military, these were words that I will always say growing up but then I didn't even have the resources I didn't even know anybody that would help me achieve that but I will just say those words with some kind of unusual conviction and certainly.

And for some reason unknown to me I just developed this big dreams and pictures of things I wanted to accomplish in my life and some of my friends then will be like Kennedy, you always say things like this, you always say you will like to travel abroad to go study, you want to join the United States military, you want to write your own book, But how are you going to make all these things happen, you do not have the financial support, your parents are not rich, you do not know anyone, how are you going to do them? But fast forward 10 years today, do you know that all those things I was saying 10 years ago have all become reality.

So here is the biggest lesson I want you to take away from this chapter, stop focusing your mind on what is wrong with you, who is not supporting you, and what is not right about your life. Instead, focus more on what you want to achieve, what you want to change and what you want to see happen in your future. That's the only thing you have control over; in other words, what matters is not where you are at the moment, what matters most is where you're going. Your direction determines your destination, your picture is your future, if you can see it in your mind, you will hold it in your hands, it's just a matter of time.

Hence, from my own little story, we can deduce that by saying those things then, earlier on in my own life, I was sowing seeds that would eventually germinate in my future i.e., I was speaking my future into existence, I was confessing what I wanted to see, not what I was seeing.

Now, let this be a reminder for you reading this, that it doesn't matter what might be going on in your life right now, what matters most is your perspective and approach towards it, wake up each day and declare what you want to see happen in your life, speak it out with confidence mixed with faith, the Bible encourages us in the book of Mark (11:24) to ask for whatever things we want in prayer and we shall have them. What that simply means is that your words have creative ability to bring about what you say, and it even goes beyond that, what you think, what you imagine, what you desire.

So, this is why it is pertinent that you begin to develop the right kind of thoughts: thoughts of positivity, thoughts of hope, thoughts of possibility, never say to yourself; I can't do it, I am not good enough, I am not strong enough, it's never going to happen to me. Instead, declare it out loud: I am the best at this, I can do it, The Lord is my helper,

I will see my dreams come through and this too shall come to pass.

The book of Genesis (1:1-14) recorded a powerful account of God's demonstration of the creative ability of the words of our mouth.

It talked about when God created the world from the beginning of time through his mouth. It reads: "The world was without form and void and God said let there be light and there was light." Note the world was without form but God overlooked the formlessness. He overlooked how chaotic the world was set up, He overlooked the darkness, instead He spoke light into existence because only He realized the creative power of his words.

God said let there be light and there was light. Note that He did not say God created, or designed, in other words, the world that we live in was created by the words that He spoke.

So, my question to you right now is, what are you speaking in your own life today? What are the things you are confessing on a daily basis?

Or are you just so focused on what is wrong and what is not working, and every day you confess negativity?

If that's your case, no problem, this might just be that reminder or that wake-up call you needed to put you back on track. It's time to shift your focus to stop speaking what you see and start speaking what you want to see.

In my own case, there was poverty, there was lack of direction, there was struggling and there was no sign of me achieving my goals, but I refused to look at those things; instead, I kept speaking what I wanted to see. That is why in this chapter, I want you to understand that you have the power to create your future.

Wrapped up within your own words is the power to change the trajectory of your life, I want you to wake up each day and declare that; "I am a child of the most High God, I'm going to see all my dreams come to pass, I am going to become all that God has made me to become, I am going to achieve my dreams, I am going to work in the best places in the world. I am blessed and highly favored." When you make words like this your everyday confession, you are invincibly setting yourself up for a glorious future.

Earlier on in my life, when I graduated from the University, I did not finish with one of the best grades in my department and so many negative thoughts dominated my mind back then. Thoughts like; you will never amount to anything with this poor grade of yours, no organization is going to hire you with this kind of result. Even one of my professors then told me, saying, "Kennedy, I have to be honest with you, with this grade you finished with, I don't think you are ever going to work in any place significant in your entire career."

But I boldly stepped out of his office and told myself, "I'm going to work in the best places in the world, I am not going to let this paper in my hands determine the great future ahead of me, I know my potential, this grade is not going to define my life." I started working on myself, I started reading books, I started investing in literature, I started attending seminars, listening to podcasts, I started reading the Bible. I chose self-development over negative thoughts, all that investment raised my self-esteem and helped me develop my communication skills, helped me develop my personality and build my confidence.

Today, I work as an Intelligence analyst with the United States Army, which is one of the strongest forces in the entire world, and not only that, I am also a published author, currently writing my third book, and recently started my own LLC too. Well, I said all that to establish the fact that I didn't let the words of my professor determine who I have become, but I chose to believe in myself and my abilities.

From believing in myself, I want you to understand that the words of your mouth have the power to create what you want to see. It is pertinent that you wake up every day and sow seeds, not only just succeeding in your own life; wake up every day, speak to your kids, declare, put your hands on their head and say, "You are going to grow up to become all you have or you are born to be, you are going to fulfill your purpose, you are going to be so great, you are smart, you're intelligent, you will do well in school." Confess positive words in the life of your children, speak positive words in your life every day. Declare, "I am going to amount to something great, irrespective of what I'm currently going through. My life is not going to end like this." The Bible acknowledges that life and death are in the power of our tongue, that we can either have life or have death through what we say.

What do you want to see in your life? Begin to speak it. It might not happen today, it might not happen tomorrow, it might not happen next month, but it will eventually happen at some point because the words of your mouth are seeds. They will germinate in time, and you will reap the harvest of your confession. Since you know that your words are seeds, what are you going to start doing every day of your life? Speak words of power, speak words of positivity, speak words of change, speak words of prosperity, and speak words of peace. Speak words of positivity, for you shall reap what you say in due time.

It is important to recognize that your words hold the power to create reality, regardless of whether they are said with intention or carelessness. Therefore, it's pertinent to be more mindful and deliberate with every word that comes out of your mouth.

Hence, here is my point: no matter what challenges you are facing right now, I encourage you to start expressing positive affirmations and envisioning a brighter future. Regardless of your current circumstances or what you may be seeing in your life, it is essential to speak words of strength, hope, and possibility. Change may not happen at once, perhaps not today or even tomorrow, but trust that, in time, the outcomes of your words will manifest in your life.

Let me share a short story from a few months ago. After finishing work, I went to pick up my car, only to discover that I had a flat tire. That day, I only had $100 with me, which was not enough to cover the repairs. For my car, but you know what? I said a little prayer: "Lord, I ask that this money will be sufficient for the tire repair, and that I will find favor with the mechanic and the staff there." I believed I would not be stranded and that I would get my car fixed.

I called my insurance, and they sent a tow truck to take my car to the mechanic. When I arrived, I was informed that the tire was beyond repair and would need to be replaced, costing $150. But I had already declared that I would find favor, and indeed, one of the managers offered to help. After I explained my situation, he kindly applied discounts and coupons, and the price was reduced to $114.

I explained that I only have $100, and to my surprise, he said, "No problem. I'll cover the difference for you this time." He mentioned that he usually would not do this, but he felt compelled to help. In that moment, my $100 was enough to get a new tire, proving the power of the affirmations I had made earlier.

This experience further reaffirms the fact that words have great power. They can shape our reality and draw positive outcomes into our lives.

My biggest question to you right now is this:

How long will you continue to remain silent and let negativity take hold of your thoughts and confessions?

Could today finally be that day you say enough is enough and start speaking words of change? And positivity into your own life. Remember, you will reap what you sow. So, speak words of power, hope, blessings, and prosperity.

Key Important Lessons:

1: Wrapped up around your words are the power to change the course of your life. If you must say something, let it be words of hope, encouragement, power, and positivity. For you shall have whatsoever you say.

2: Your tongue is the tiniest part of your body, but it carries with it the energy, power, and capacity to utter the trajectory of your life. Therefore, you must be intentionally selective about what you say, not just to yourself but also to others.

3: Your words are seeds; choose them carefully because they will bring to pass your most dominant confessions. In other words, every time you speak, you are either sowing seeds of hope or fear, seeds of triumph or defeat, seeds of encouragement or seeds of despair. You shall have what you say in time.

Biblical Reflection:

The tongue can bring death or life; those who love to talk will reap the consequences.

Proverbs 18:21– NLT.

Winning Wisdom 6: You Are Enough

"You are good enough, smart enough, beautiful enough, and strong enough. You just must believe it."

KK KING

Today, we live in a world where everyone is constantly trying to prove themselves, constantly trying to compare themselves with others. It is very easy to lose one's self-worth when you don't instantly gain the accolades and appreciation you seek from the outside world. But I want to remind you that, from the day you were born, you were inherently born with your self-worth. The Creator God wouldn't have even thought of creating you in the first place if He didn't know you were worthy to be here.

In other words, there is nothing you are going to do today or even tomorrow that will increase your worthiness. God has already made you significant; your life has a value embedded in it from birth, your opinions matter, your existence here in this world today shows that you are also a part of this big thing called the universe.

The world needs your ideas, the world needs your skills, the world needs your own unique contribution. In fact, the world would be incomplete without you in it.

Never underestimate the power and significance you bring to the world. If you've ever doubted your worth or intelligence, let me remind you: you are valuable, you are needed, and you have a unique role to play.

Stop seeking external validation; recognize that true validation comes from within. If you don't receive applause from others, applaud yourself. If you lack encouragement, be your own cheerleader. If appreciation seems absent, learn to appreciate yourself. Thank yourself daily, look in the mirror, and give yourself a pat on the back. Say aloud, "I am capable, I am smart, and I deserve all the good life has to offer."

One of the most important lessons I've learned is that you cannot succeed by trying to please everyone. Not everyone will appreciate you, and that's perfectly fine. What matters is that you recognize your own strengths and achievements. It's essential to reflect on how far you've come in life. It can be tempting to compare yourself to others, but remember, you were born to measure your growth against your past self, not others.

Reflect on where you were five years ago. While you may not have accomplished everything you aspired to, you are not where you once were. You've made progress. Revisit the goals you set; you will often find that many have been achieved. Acknowledge your growth. Celebrate your efforts by telling yourself, "Yes, I'm trying. I am better today. I am enough." Remind yourself that everything will align in due time.

Be kind to yourself. Accept yourself and love yourself; this is the foundation of progress. Your worth is not something to be earned; it has been innately a part of you since the day you were born. There is nothing you can do today to diminish your worth; you are magnificent just as you are.

The right people in your life will see your value. Stop searching for validation or worrying about who likes you; not everyone will appreciate you. Ultimately, you are worthy simply by being you, and those meant to be in your life will recognize and embrace you for who you truly are. A short story about an Artist Named Elara.

Once upon a time in a small village, there lived an artist named Elara. She poured her heart into her paintings, expressing her emotions and experiences through vibrant colors and intricate strokes. However, despite her passion, she often hesitated to share her art with the world, fearing it would never be good enough.

Elara would frequently visit the local marketplace, where she observed other artists showcasing their work. She admired their skill and confidence but felt a gnawing sense of inadequacy. "If only my paintings were as beautiful as theirs," she would think. Those thoughts held her back, trapping her in a cycle of self-doubt.

One sunny afternoon, an elderly man came to the marketplace. He was known for his wisdom and kindness. As he walked past Elara's booth, he stopped and gazed at her paintings. The colors danced on the canvas, each stroke a testament to her feelings and experiences. Elara held her breath, fearing judgment.

Tell me, young artist," the man said gently, "what does your heart express through these colors?"

Elara hesitated but eventually replied, "I just want to create beautiful art, but I fear it's not enough compared to others."

The man smiled warmly and replied, "Beauty lies not in perfection but in authenticity. Your art reflects your soul, your journey, and that in itself is enough. Embrace your unique voice; it is what the world needs."

With those words, something shifted within Elara. She realized that her worth wasn't dependent on comparisons. Her art was an extension of herself, and it didn't need to resemble anyone else's. That evening, she decided to hang her paintings proudly for all to see, her heart swelling with newfound confidence.

As the days passed, Elara's work began to draw attention. People were enthralled not only by the colors but also by the emotion captured in every piece. They felt a connection to her story and authenticity. Elara learned that by accepting and celebrating her unique perspective, she could touch lives and inspire others.

Hence, Elara's story reminds us that we each have our unique journey to share, and it's crucial to acknowledge that we are enough in our authentic selves. Embracing who we are allows us to express ourselves more freely and deeply, creating connections that resonate with others.

So, let's embark on this journey of self-acceptance. Celebrate your individuality, acknowledge your strengths, and remember you are enough, just as you are. Your presence in this world is valued, and your contributions matter. Embrace the beauty of being you.

You are one unique individual in a room of a million, be unapologetically you! You are enough.

Key important Lessons:

1. You were originally created to stand out, stop trying to fit in.

2. You are not going to be liked and appreciated by everyone, no matter what you do, and that is okay.

"We do not dare to classify or compare ourselves with some who commend themselves. When they measure themselves by themselves and compare themselves with themselves, they are not wise."

–Corinthians 10:12–

Winning Wisdom 7: Overcoming Limiting Beliefs

"There are really no limitations in the world except the ones we create in our minds."

Odimba k

Some of the biggest problems we face in life are the beliefs we have about ourselves, beliefs about what is possible for us to accomplish, and beliefs about the way we think things are.

Which is completely different from the way things actually are. In other words, by changing some of our beliefs, we can tentatively begin to change our lives.

And this is true if applied in our relationships, physical health and life vocations. It's not the way things are that really affects us, but the way we think they are that actually does.

Let me share a little story about how I grew up, to help you set some perspective on how you can also apply this concept in your own personal life.

I am the first child in a family of five, which consists of three brothers and one sister. I grew up in a very modest family, which lacked so many advantages that some of my peers had growing up.

What you may consider a very humble beginning, my parents struggled to raise my siblings and me, but I never let my background or family struggles stop me from having big dreams, and what changed for me was exposing myself to good books and reading the Bible very early in my life.

I have always believed, and I still believe that the Bible is one of the most important books in the world.

And this mindset or perspective made me think completely differently from my peers, and that transformed mindset helped me to discover the power of setting goals, having a vision for my future, and the power of positive thinking.

Hence, one of the core limitations that were very significant in my family bloodline growing up was the inability of anyone going past high school, and that became like a stereotype, for so many years in my family.

Knowing this however, made me even more determined to be the first person to break that limit, which I finally did in 2011, when I became the first person in my family to obtain a college degree. It was not easy, but I did it through courage and a belief that nothing is impossible when you set your mind on it. And today we have over 10 family members who are all college graduates, but it took one person to prove that it was possible, irrespective of the prevailing family circumstances.

Today, I work with the United States Army, I am a published author in one of the finest countries in the world, and I am currently working on my second book, while raising my 7-year-old son as a single dad.

This is where things that were never thought possible ten years ago by me, looking back, I would say it was made possible because I changed the way I viewed life, and I believe life is all about perspective, in other words, if you think something is possible, you are right, and if you think otherwise, you often are not wrong too.

You see, there are really no limits to what we can accomplish in life except for the limits we place on ourselves. Simply put, change your mindset and your life will follow suit.

In other words, you alone have the power to change the narrative of your life by changing the way you interpret the events of your life.

Here is my point: by changing your thinking, you can change the outcome of your life, and that is why I have shared some of the biggest lessons I have learned over these years in my first Book Tilted: Living Beyond Limitations Everyday.

And if you haven't already read my first book, I do recommend you check it out as well.

Key Important Lessons:

1. You must believe in yourself and never doubt your abilities. Because you are stronger and even smarter than you think you are.

2. Each one of you can do great things, and that does not mean you will not fail at some point in your career. But you must understand that life is not measured in falling; it's measured in getting back up each time you fall.

3. Embrace your uniqueness and never compare yourself with anyone. Because your personal power lies in your uniqueness.

Biblical References:

I can do all things through Christ who strengthens me

Philippians 4:13–

Winning Wisdom 8: The What-If Factor

Fearlessness and Trust

Fearlessness is about trusting your instincts and maintaining clarity of thought. Once you've made a decision, don't let the "What-ifs" hold you back. As Ravi Shastri reminds us, the "What-if" factor is a significant barrier that prevents many people from achieving their dreams.

The Barrier of Doubt

The reality is that you and I are often more capable, more intelligent, stronger, and more creative than we realize.

Hence, repeatedly, people are hindered by questions like, "What if I'm not good enough?" or "What if I fail?" These doubts can paralyze us, preventing progress. Ironically, we rarely pause to ask ourselves, "What if I succeed?" or what if it all works out?

We tend to focus on the negative aspects of our potential, allowing ourselves to become immobilized by fear. One of the most important lessons I've learned throughout my writing career and life journey is that, you never truly know how strong or powerful you are until you take the leap.

You see the reality is that, you're usually more talented than you think, but you are often hindered by the negative thoughts and beliefs you have about yourself.

Here is my point, you have got to Trust Yourself!

Whatever you aspire to do in life, overcoming the mental blocks that prevent you from trusting yourself is essential. You must believe in your abilities and your worthiness to turn your dreams into reality. Consider Mark Zuckerberg, the creator of Facebook. If he had doubted himself and let fear dictate his choices, we might not have the social connectivity we enjoy today. The platform he created allows people to communicate and share content globally, all because he overcame the mental barriers of "What if it doesn't work?"

Here comes my questions to you:

What dreams or ideas lie dormant in your mind?

God may have instilled a vision in you; whether it's writing a book, composing music, or developing an app. Are you allowing fear to rob you of the chance to bring these ideas to life? Instead of worrying about failure, or what if no one supports you. Instead, ask yourself how you can take that first step towards bringing your dreams to reality.

One of my biggest discoveries in life is that you can never know what you can do or create until you try, and just in case you try and fail, try again and again until you succeed!

Here is the fact.

Everything we enjoy today, from airplanes to smartphones, was brought into existence by those who dared to believe in their potential. I urge you to recognize your capability. You are equipped with everything you need to manifest your dreams. If you can conceive an idea, you can create it. The Bible states in Matthew that we have the power to bring our thoughts into reality.

Believe in Yourself

Never let negative thoughts or the opinions of others deter you from pursuing your dreams. You are talented enough, and you possess the skills necessary to succeed. John C. Maxwell once said that, "If we do all we are capable of, we will amaze ourselves." You are capable of so much more than you may realize.

Taking the First Step

You don't need all the resources or knowledge to begin. The crucial step is to start, and once you do, everything will begin to align. For instance, I grew up in Nigeria with a strong desire to study in the United States, despite coming from a poor family with limited resources. My parents were skeptical and lacked the means to support my dream. However, I believed in my purpose and took action. I searched for schools and applied to New York State University.

Against the odds, I was accepted, even though I faced challenges in funding my education.

Key important lessons:

1. The journey to realizing your dreams often begins with overcoming doubt and taking that first step. Trust yourself and your abilities.

2. You have everything inside you to turn your ideas into reality. Don't let fear dictate your path. Instead, embrace the possibilities and believe that you can achieve greatness.

Biblical Reflection:

"I can do all this through him who gives me strength." - Philippians 4:13-

Winning Wisdom 9: What is your Why?

"Your why is the driving force that keeps you going when things get tough."

Kennedy King

The question "What is your why?" is one of the most important questions you must ask yourself. It has been said that if you know your "Why," you will find your "How". Motivational speaker and Author Simon Sinek said it even better, he said.

"People don't just buy what you sell; they buy why you sell it."

You see, it's crucial to understand the why of your life. As someone once said, there are two significant events in your life: the day you were born and the day you discover your WHY.

Understanding your purpose is one of the most vital things you will uncover, especially during challenging times when things get tough. What keeps you motivated? What drives you forward? It's your "why." If you truly know your purpose, nothing can stop you. Your is what keeps you awake when others are asleep, I still remember times I have to wake up very early to write my book, and this is a book I worked on for over 10 years, it wasn't comfortable, it wasn't easy, there were times I even thought of giving up on the project, but I kept reminding myself the main reason why I started writing in the first place. And that was my desire to contribute my little knowledge towards making the world better than I met it.

You see, growing up, I was mostly influenced by books and authors I have listened to speak at different events.

I asked questions; I ask myself how can I use what I have learned over the years to influence the next generation, young people who look up to me for guidance, and in order not to disappoint them, I have to fight even on the days I was tired to make sure I completed my book.

And this is exactly what I mean by you discovering your own WHY, because that's the only driving force and motivation that will keep you going when things get tough. And they will, but if you have a very strong WHY on those difficult days, nothing can stop you because you always find enough reasons to keep pushing you forward irrespective of what is in your way.

Let me remind you of your "Why." Why did you start in the first place? Why did you decide to pursue an education? Why did you want to learn a new skill or start a new program? Why did you choose to change your life? I want you to realize that you are capable and strong. You have the potential to achieve everything you are meant to be in this world. Ask yourself, "Why did I start this?" At that moment, a new revelation, a new power, and a renewed vision will awaken within.

You are born for impact, for a legacy, and to change your world. Never let temporary obstacles hinder you from fulfilling the potential God has bestowed upon you. You are destined for greatness, and you have come too far to stop now.

Let me share a little background story about my experience growing up as a teenager.

This happened when I was trying to gain admission into college. I have also shared this story on one of my live sessions on Facebook. If you follow me on there, you must have come across it, but if you haven't seen it, I encourage you to check it out.

Before starting university, I told myself I would be the first person in my family to earn a college degree, and that was my biggest WHY.

You see, growing up, there was a stereotype that no one in my family bloodline could achieve much beyond high school. This is something that has lingered in my family for so many years, but when I reached the point where I wanted to attend college, I resolved to break that limit and become the first to obtain a degree.

But it was not easy. The first time I applied to attend college, I was accepted and passed all the entrance exams, but I could not afford the tuition. I missed the deadline and lost my admission. But guess what? I did not give up, though. The second time, I was accepted again, but still lacked support, and once more, I lost my admission.

But I stayed resilient because I had a WHY, and that kept me grounded.

By the third attempt, my aunt began to question my persistence. She asked, "Why do you keep trying? Even when no one has supported you before." But because I had a strong "why," I refused to give up.

I tried again, and this time, I was accepted to study philosophy. Miraculously, my uncle, who lives in another country, heard about my acceptance. He offered to help me, despite not having spoken to me for so many years. I didn't even know how he got the news, but that's what happens when your mind is made up for what you want out of life, I mean when you refuse to accept defeat, when you keep pushing forward irrespective of the facts of life. Because if you do not give up, there is always a point where your efforts will pay off. Where opportunity meets preparation. And that was my case.

My uncle even had to sell some of his possessions to raise money for my tuition and expenses.

With his support, I was able to attend school for four years and earn my degree. I became the first person in my family to graduate from college.

I refused to give up because I was motivated by my "Why."

Here is my point: when your "Why" is strong enough, nothing can stop you from realizing your dreams. You will see doors suddenly opening from places you never thought of, therefore, before you quit, think about why you started in the first place. Stay lifted and remember that you are stronger and more capable than you think. Let your faith be greater than your fears, and let your "Why" overshadow your limitations. There is always a light at the end of the tunnel. You got this!

Key important lessons:

1. When your why is clear enough from the beginning, your how will manifest itself.

2. The problem in life is not worrying about whether you are going to fall, because you will fall at some point in your journey to uncover your path in life, but the biggest challenge is having enough WHY to get you back up when you fall.

Biblical Reflection:

Commit to the Lord whatever you do, and he will establish   your plans."

Proverbs 16:3-

Wining Wisdom 10: You Are Unique

"You were created uniquely; there is no one like you in the entire world, and there will never be anyone else that will be created with your exact features, even in centuries to come."

Odimba K

You have a unique assignment to fulfill in the world.

In other words, there is something about you that sets you apart from your colleagues, friends, and even siblings, which is not a limitation; it's your power place, and that is why you do not have to compare yourself with anyone else.

Just the other day, I took my 5-year-old son to a park near my house to play with some other kids, and as he began playing, he got so attached to one particular kid among them, and when it was about time for us to leave, I called his attention and said son! It's about time for us to leave, but in hesitance, he said Daddy can you give me some more time?

I said ok, I will give you 10 more minutes to play with your friends okay.

Immediately, he ran to one of his friend, which he seems to prefer among the other ones, and said to her, my daddy said we will be leaving in 10 minutes but I am worried that I may not be able to recognize you next time I see you.

I lean in to grasp what they were saying to each other and to my greatest surprise the little 5-year-old responded, no you will recognize me because I will be putting on the same shoes I have on now, but my son insisted, saying no I will still not be able to recognize you even if you put on the same shoes.

The little 5-year-old gave a second response that completely changed my whole perspective about how the original creator God wired us as humans.

She said, "You will still be able to recognize me because of my face, nobody looks like me." And I was like wow! What could have made this little 5-year-old little girl think this way?

Where did she learn this perspective from? What if every one of us can think and view life from this perspective? Won't that be a gamechanger? In the way we relate to each other?

I mean a realization that no one in the world looks exactly like you, that you are unique, and that you will be recognized no matter the number of people around you.

Won't this knowledge change the way we approach our lives and ultimately put an end to comparison and the quest to fit in or be liked by a certain group of people? Yes or no?

Here is my point, it is therefore pertinent for you to realize that your ideas, wisdom, creativity, and personality were all crafted by God to enable you to fulfill your assignment in this world.

This includes your passions, interests, urges, looks, and every detail of your personal reality. There is, therefore, no place for comparison with others. You are unique! You are special!

I hope this reality rings like a bell in your heart that awakens your greatness and helps you take your place in the world.

You are something new to the world. Never, since the beginning of time, has there ever been anybody exactly like you, and never again throughout all the ages to come, will there ever be anybody exactly like you again.

You are incomparable, you are something new in the face of the earth, the world has never seen anything like you before and the world will never see anything like you again, even after you have left this earthly existence.

Therefore, be bold and approach this life with confidence, knowing that your ideas count, your presence is needed, the world needs your own unique genius, and that you are that one piece needed to complete the puzzle. You are valuable!

In other words, you were created uniquely; you are not here by random selection. You are here because you were meant to be here. And there is a unique purpose you are here to fulfill. Your life has a unique significance; never let anyone's opinion of you make you feel less of yourself.

Key important lessons:

1. You must believe in yourself and never doubt your abilities. Because you are stronger and even smarter than you think you are.

2. Everyone can do wonderful things, and that does not mean you will not fail at some point in your career. But you must understand that life is not measured in falling; it's measured in getting back up each time you fall.

3. Embrace your uniqueness and never compare yourself with anyone. Because your personal power lies in your uniqueness, stand out and be unapologetically different!

Biblical Reflection

"I praise you, for I am fearfully and wonderfully made.
Wonderful are your works; my soul knows it very well

-Psalm 139:14-

Winning Wisdom 11: Adversity Has Advantages

"In every defeat you face in life is always a hidden lesson that has within it, the keys to do better next time."

Kennedy King

Every Adversity has its advantages; this is a profound topic worth exploring in depth.

The Bible even says that we should consider it joy when we face trials and tribulations, as these experiences test our patience. Challenges and life's adversities serve as a purification process, preparing us for what lies ahead. Everything we enjoy today, everything we see, has emerged from overcoming obstacles. Without facing problems, how would we know how to devise solutions?

When you find yourself in adversity, it's not meant to bring you down or to destroy you; rather, it's designed to make you a better, stronger, and more creative person. Instead of asking, "Why is this happening to me?" consider reframing the question to, "What can I learn from this experience?" Instead of self-blame, recognize that challenges often unlock your potential, fostering creativity and innovation.

Take, for instance, the story of Thomas Edison, who famously said he failed over a hundred times before inventing the light bulb. Each failure brought him closer to understanding what didn't work, ultimately leading him to discover the solution that revolutionized the world. Had he given up, we might not have electricity today.

In our own lives, we will inevitably face trials, disappointments, and delays. Adversity is a part of life, and failure is an integral aspect of success. It's through failure that we learn and discover better ways to approach problems. Instead of seeing failure as a setback, view it as a stepping stone toward growth and improvement.

I can relate personally to this journey. Initially, I aimed to study in Australia. I was accepted into an economics program at a prestigious university, but faced a significant obstacle: I lacked the funds to pay my tuition. Despite my efforts to secure a loan and work extra jobs, I missed the payment deadline and lost my opportunity. This was a significant blow, yet I didn't give up. A year later, I applied to study in the UK, only to face another setback with a missed deadline.

During this challenging period, I turned to God for guidance. The adversity I faced drew me closer to my faith and helped me realize that I was not alone in my struggles. It was during this time that I received a revelation: I was meant to go to the U.S. With renewed purpose, I applied for a visa, and everything began to align. I secured the necessary funds, went through the interview process, and was accepted.

Reflecting on this journey, I can see how adversity has shaped me. It taught me resilience and creativity and revealed the support I had from unexpected sources. Today, I've been living in the U.S. for over ten years, and I'm grateful for the path that brought me here.

The key takeaway is that whatever challenges you face are not meant to destroy you but to help you grow. The Bible reminds us that all things work together for good for those who love God. Your current struggles, be it illness, heartbreak, or disappointment, will ultimately serve a purpose. They can become your testimony and a source of strength for others facing similar challenges.

Do not be discouraged; everyone encounters adversity at some point in life. It's through these experiences that we can uncover the glory within us and emerge stronger. Be patient through your trials, as patience produces perseverance and character. You are greater than your circumstances. What is meant for you is far more significant than what stands against you.

Remember, this too shall pass. Your struggles will come to an end. You will emerge stronger, more creative, and equipped to help others. Don't give up; embrace your journey through adversity.

Key important lessons:

1: Adversity or life challenges are not meant to destroy you; they are actually meant to make you stronger, smarter and well-equipped to face the journey of life ahead of you.

2: It is in the midst of your adversity that you will discover your true strength that is required to fulfill your life's divine purpose. Problems reveal you to your true identity and hidden abilities.

3: Adversity helps you tap into the divine powers of your Creator God, because it forces you to seek guidance out of your own abilities, which is needed for your journey in life.

Bible reference:

Consider it pure joy my brothers and sisters, whenever you face trials of many kinds, because you know that the testing of your faith produces perseverance. Let perseverance finish its work so that you may be mature and complete, not lacking anything.

- James 1:2-4 -

Winning Wisdom 12: Every Problem Has a Solution

"Don't be too quick to quit on your dreams yet. Because the things you are looking for are usually revealed in unexpected ways and times."

Kennedy King

If you are reading these words right now, pause for a moment and breathe.

The fact that you have made it this far means something powerful: you refused to quit. You chose growth over comfort, faith over fear, and hope over surrender. Many start the journey; few stay long enough to be transformed. Your presence here is proof that something greater is working within you.

From the beginning of this journey, you learned that you are not defined by your circumstances. You discovered that the power to change your life does not live outside of you, it lives within you. You are unique, intentional, and created with purpose. Along the way, we explored keys, attitudes, and daily approaches designed to awaken the greatness already placed inside you.

As we arrive at this final chapter, I want to leave you with one unshakable truth: Every problem has a solution.

Life tests us most when we feel least prepared. Challenges rise, answers delay, and doubt begins to whisper. In those moments, giving up can feel easier than pressing forward. That is why this chapter matters, because your life is not stuck; your perspective is. When you change the way you see things, things begin to change for you.

Problems exist, but they were never meant to destroy you. They were meant to develop you. Everything rises and falls on mindset. When you learn to see life through a possibility mindset, doors open where walls once stood.

God did not create you empty. He created you with potential, resilience, and divine capacity. Often, the clearest lessons come from the simplest places.

One of the most powerful lessons I ever learned came from my son.

One day, I bought my son a small racing car toy, something simple, but special to him. While I studied for my exams, he played. Later, he took a nap. When he woke up, the toy was gone.

He searched and searched, then came to me and said, "Daddy, I can't find my toy."

I got up and helped him. We searched every room, every corner. After several minutes, I told him I would buy another one. He sat quietly for a moment. Then he stood up, looked at me, and said words that shifted my spirit:

"I'm not going to give up. I'm going to find my toy."

At seven years old, he understood what many adults forget: Giving up is a choice, not a destiny.

He searched again, this time with belief. He checked the back door, the laundry room, and the kitchen. There, under the kitchen table, he found his toy. He came running, shouting, "Daddy, I found it! I told you I wouldn't give up!"

In that moment, God spoke to me through my child. Now, I ask you: what are you about to give up on? Is it a dream delayed?

A calling that feels distant?

A business that hasn't grown yet?

A healing you are still believing for? A silent battle no one else sees?

This is not the end.

Say it aloud if you can:

"I will not give up."

"I've come too far to stop now." "I will finish what I started." Heaven responds to persistence.

Sometimes your breakthrough is not found in quitting, but in taking one more step. Sometimes the answer is in the next phone call, the next email, the next conversation, or the next act of obedience. Sometimes God is simply asking you to step out of your comfort zone so He can reveal another way.

Every problem has a solution. At times, the solution is not an immediate change; it is endurance.

One morning on my way to work, traffic was completely blocked. Police were everywhere. Time was slipping away, and frustration filled the air. Everyone waited, stuck and discouraged.

Then I made a decision, I turned around.

In that moment, I discovered a route I had never taken before. Because my mind was conditioned to one way, I had never seen the other. That new route took me to work right on time.

Sometimes God is waiting for you to turn, not because you are wrong, but because there is another way.

You may be focusing on one solution when there are many. Change your mindset. Ask questions. Seek wisdom. Talk to someone. Pray. Research. Move forward.

It is too late to quit now.

As I close this book, my prayer is that these words settle deeply into your spirit. If you have come this far, you were meant to. Your solution is closer than you think.

Hold on.

Trust God.

Do not give up.

There is a solution to your problem and it is already on its way.

Key important lessons:

1. The solutions you are looking for are sometimes closer than you think, you just must hold on a little longer. It might just be the next phone call you make or receive or the next door you open, or even the next handshake to that stranger next to you. Keep your hope alive. This too will happen.

2. Every problem carries within it the seed of greatness; sometimes all you can do is go through the problem to enjoy the potential fruits that are hidden within it.

3. Do not try to rush out of the problem, for within it lies the keys to your greatness.

"Is anything too difficult or too wonderful for the Lord? At the appointed time, when the season [for her delivery] comes, I will return to you, and Sarah will have a son.

-Genesis 18:14-

20 Profound Quotes from Kennedy Odimba

1. You wouldn't know what you can do until you try.

2. It is not what you go through in life that changes your life, but what you do with the lessons learned that does.

3. It's the little disciplines practiced daily in secret that produce the results that everyone celebrates.

4. You were created for more. Don't just exist, make an impact.

5. Your fears are not real, they are made-up negative pictures created by your own mind. Don't cross your bridges until you come to them.

6. You are incomparable, you are something new on the face of the earth, the world has never seen anything like you before. And the world will never see anything like you again after you have lived through this earth and gone. Be authentic.

7. Count your blessings, not your troubles.

8. The moment you replace negative thoughts with positive thoughts, you will start having positive results.

9. When you do your part, God will do his part.

10. You may not be able to change the wind, the rain, the seasons and times, but you have the power to change

yourself.

11. Who you are is not what other people think or say about you; who you are is fundamentally determined by the way you think and feel about yourself.

12. Believe in your ideas, you wouldn't have thought of it in the first place, if you didn't already have the ability to bring them to fruition.

13. Take the first step in faith, you don't have to see the whole staircase, just take the first step.

14. When you think about quitting, also think about why you started.

15. 16, In a fast-changing world that we live in right now, the biggest questions are no longer about what you know; the biggest questions are more about what you can learn?

16. It's better to die in the war of chasing your dreams than to live kneeling to your fears.

17. You can't experience in reality what you have not first experienced in your mind.

18. Your success will largely be determined by your own self-confidence and belief in your abilities.

19. You become rich in your mind long before you become rich in your bank account. Normalize thinking big.

20. Your biggest dreams will take time, you just have to remain consistent. Set your eyes on the goal, not the process.

About the Author

Kennedy King Odimba is a motivational speaker, life coach, philosopher and currently works for the United States Army as a Chaplain Assistance.

He is dedicated to helping people rise above limitations and live with purpose, confidence, and faith.

He is the author of "Living Beyond Limitations Every Day", which has sold thousands of copies around the world.

Hence, in "Designed for Victory", he dives in even deeper into reminding us how powerful and superior God has made us over life circumstances.

Originally from Nigeria, Kennedy has lived in the United States for over ten years. His journey from humble beginnings to building a life of impact continues to inspire audiences across different backgrounds, bringing discipline, resilience, and strategic thinking into his work as a coach and speaker.

He is also a co-host for the primetime podcast that airs every Thursday on his YouTube channel, where he discusses mindset, purpose, faith, and personal growth.

Kennedy currently lives in Nashville, Tennessee, where he continues to write, speak, coach, and empower others to live intentionally and victoriously.

To learn more about Kennedy's work and stay connected, follow him on:

- Facebook: Kennedy King
- YouTube: King's Solutions Network
- Instagram: @KennedyKing_coaching
- Website: www.KingsSolutionsNetwork.com

Do not forget to subscribe, follow, and share Kennedy's work with your loved ones.